RUBANK EDUCATIONAL LIBRARY No. 62

Soloist Folio

FOR
TROMBONE or BARITONE ∶

T0078859

with Piano Accompaniment

CONTENTS

RUBANK ®

HAL•LEONARD ®
CORPORATION
7777 W. BLUEMOUND RD. P.O. BOX 13819 MILWAUKEE, WI 53213

SONG OF ² THE SUN

BALLAD

EDWARD C. BARROLL

Copyright Renewed

Copyright MCMXXVIII by Rubank Inc., Chicago, Ill.
International Copyright Secured

B Agitato *(faster)*

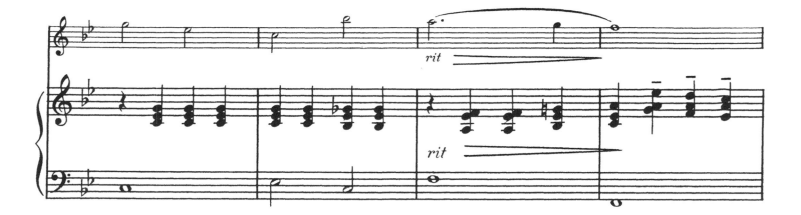

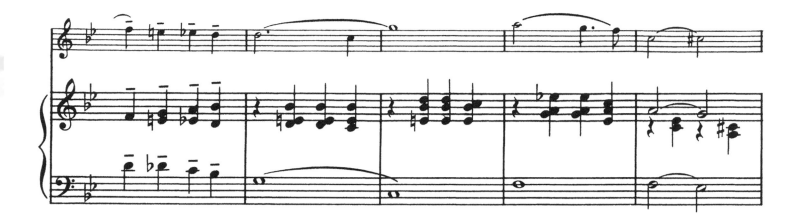

BRILLIANT POLKA

E. De LAMATER

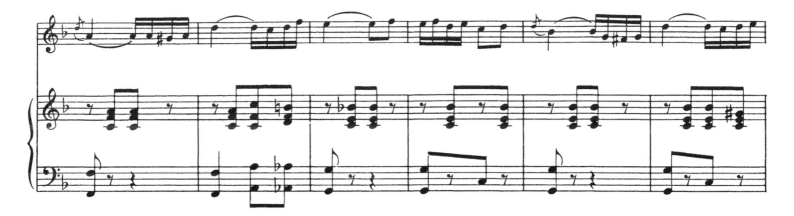

Copyright MCMXXXII by Rubank Inc., Chicago, Ill.
International Copyright Secured

Copyright Renewed

Moderato *with expression*

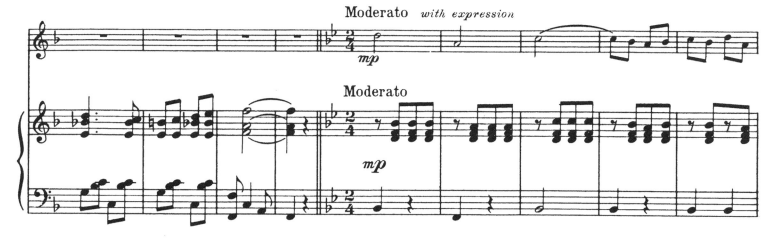

Moderato

Brilliant Polka

Moderato

D. S.

⊕ CODA *faster*

⊕ CODA

mf faster

Brilliant Polka

THOUGHTS OF HOME

BALLAD

E. DE LAMATER

Allegro Moderato

PIANO

Copyright Renewed

Copyright MCMXXXII by Rubank Inc. Chicago, Ill.
International Copyright Secured

Thoughts of Home

Thoughts of Home

Dedicated to all my friends

FRIENDS

WALTZ CAPRICE

CLAY SMITH

Waltz tempo

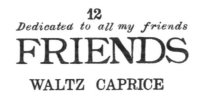

Tempo di Valse

Copyright Renewed

Copyright MCMXXXI by Rubank Inc., Chicago, Ill.
International Copyright Secured

Friends

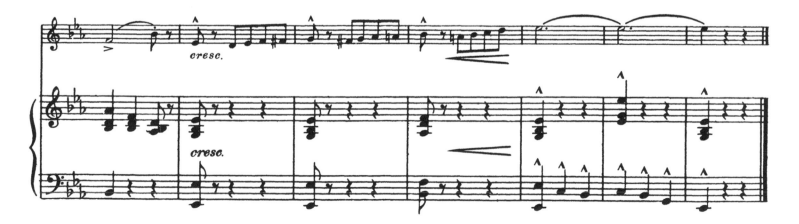

Friends

Melody from

Concerto in B♭ Minor

Piano

PETER I. TSCHAIKOWSKY
Arr. by Herman A. Hummel

Copyright MCMXLI by Rubank, Inc., Chicago, Ill.
International Copyright Secured
Copyright Renewed

Piano

EMERALD
Progressive Solos for Trombone or Baritone

VANDER COOK

Andante

Copyright Renewed

Copyright MCMXXXVIII by Rubank Inc., Chicago, Ill.
International Copyright Secured

Moderato

TRIO

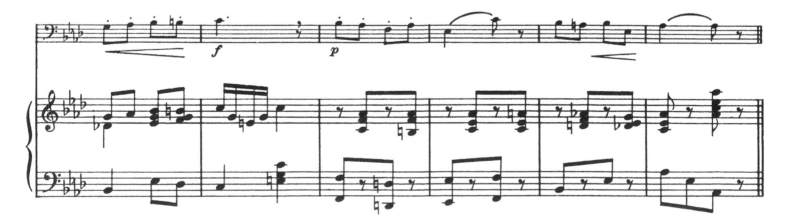

Emerald

Emerald

ROMANCE

E. De Lamater

Copyright Renewed

Copyright MCMXXXII by Rubank Inc., Chicago, Ill.
International Copyright Secured

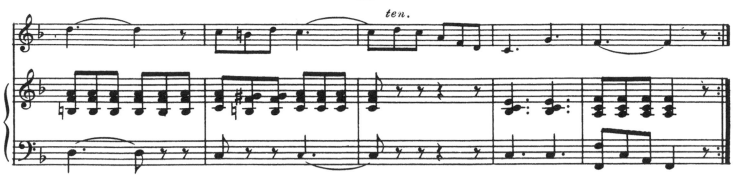

Agitato *faster*

broad

Tempo I

rubato a tempo

Romance

CONGRATULATIONS

WALTZ CAPRICE

E. DE LAMATER

Copyright Renewed

Copyright MCMXXXI by Rubank Inc., Chicago, Ill.
International Copyright Secured

RUBANK EDUCATIONAL LIBRARY No. 62

Soloist Folio

FOR
TROMBONE or BARITONE 𝄢
with Piano Accompaniment

CONTENTS

RUBANK®

HAL•LEONARD®
CORPORATION
7777 W. BLUEMOUND RD. P.O. BOX 13819 MILWAUKEE, WI 53213

SONG OF THE SUN
BALLAD

EDWARD C. BARROLL

Copyright Renewed

Copyright MCMXXXI by Rubank, Inc., Chicago, Ill.
International Copyright Secured

BRILLIANT POLKA

Trombone or Baritone

E. De LAMATER

Copyright Renewed

Copyright MCMXXXII by Rubank Inc., Chicago, Ill.
International Copyright Secured

THOUGHTS OF HOME

BALLAD

Trombone or Baritone

E. DE LAMATER

A cut may be made from A to B

Copyright Renewed

Copyright MCMXXXII by Rubank Inc., Chicago, Ill.
International Copyright Secured

FRIENDS

WALTZ CAPRICE

CLAY SMITH

Solo Trombone ♪:
or Baritone

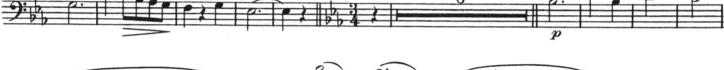

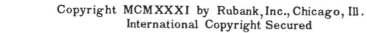

Copyright Renewed

Copyright MCMXXXI by Rubank, Inc., Chicago, Ill.
International Copyright Secured

6
Melody from
Concerto in B♭ Minor

Trombone - Baritone 𝄢 (Solo)

PETER I. TSCHAIKOWSKY
Arr. by Herman A. Hummel

Copyright Renewed

Copyright MCMXLI by Rubank, Inc., Chicago, Ill.
International Copyright Secured

EMERALD

VANDER COOK

Copyright Renewed

Copyright MCMXXXVIII by Rubank Inc., Chicago, Ill.
International Copyright Secured

8
ROMANCE

Trombone or Baritone 𝄢

E. DeLAMATER

Copyright Renewed

Copyright MCMXXXII by Rubank Inc., Chicago, Ill.
International Copyright Secured

CONGRATULATIONS

WALTZ CAPRICE

Trombone or Baritone 𝄢

Waltz tempo

E. DE LAMATER

Copyright Renewed

Copyright MCMXXXI by Rubank, Inc., Chicago, Ill.
International Copyright Secured

Cantique de Noel

Solo Trombone 𝄢
or Baritone

ADOLPHE ADAM
Transcribed by G.E. Holmes

Copyright Renewed

Copyright MCMXXXIX by Rubank Inc., Chicago, Ill.
International Copyright Secured

The Holy City

Solo Trombone 𝄢
or Baritone

STEPHEN ADAMS
Arr. by E. DeLamater

Andante moderato

Soloist Folio   Copyright MCMXLIV by Rubank, Inc., Chicago   Copyright Renewed

Carnival of Venice

Air Varie

Trombone

HENRY W. DAVIS

Copyright Renewed

Copyright MCMXLII by Rubank, Inc., Chicago, Ill.
International Copyright Secured

Trombone

GLEN EDEN[14]
POLKA

Range

Trombone
Baritone 𝄢

CHAS. W. STORM

Allegro maestoso

Andante — Solo — *mf*

TUTTI *f* — *Cadenza*

POLKA *mf*

rit. — *a tempo*

TUTTI — *Fine*

Solo — *mf D. S. al Fine*

Copyright Renewed

Copyright MCMXXXIII by Rubank Inc., Chicago, Ill.
International Copyright Secured

15
Trombone & Baritone

Stupendo

Concert Polka

Trombone or Baritone Solo

N. K. BRAHMSTEDT

Copyright MCMXXXVII by Rubank Inc., Chicago, Ill.
International Copyright Secured
Copyright Renewed

Congratulations

Congratulations

Cantique de Noel

ADOLPHE ADAM
Transcribed by G. E. Holmes

Andante

(10)

Copyright Renewed

Copyright MCMXXXIX by Rubank Inc.,Chicago, Ill.
International Copyright Secured

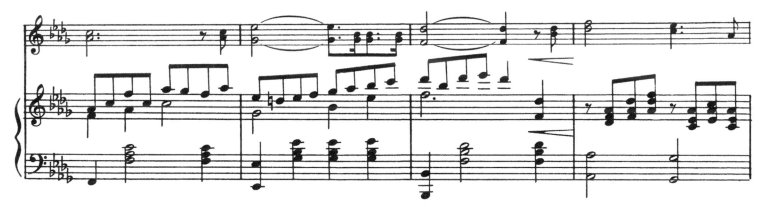

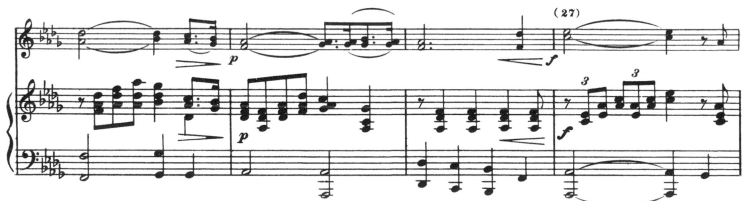

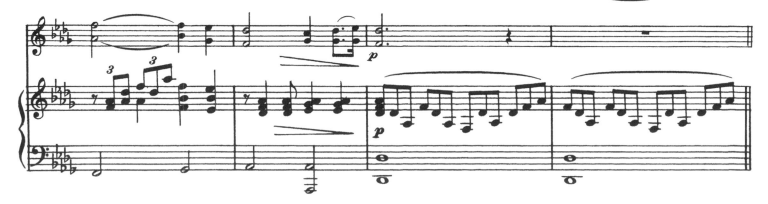

Cantique de Noel

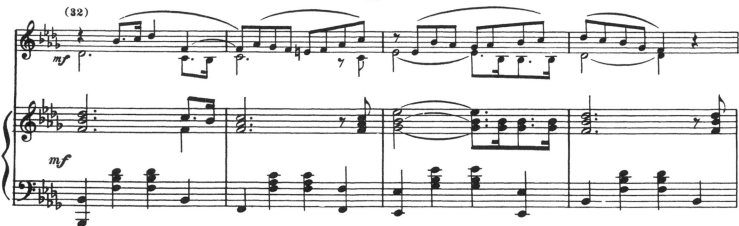

Cantique de Noel

30
THE HOLY CITY

Solo or Duet for Cornet, Trombone
Clarinet and Alto Saxophone

STEPHEN ADAMS
Arr. by E. DeLamater

Copyright MCM XLIV by Rubank, Inc., Chicago, Ill.
Copyright Renewed

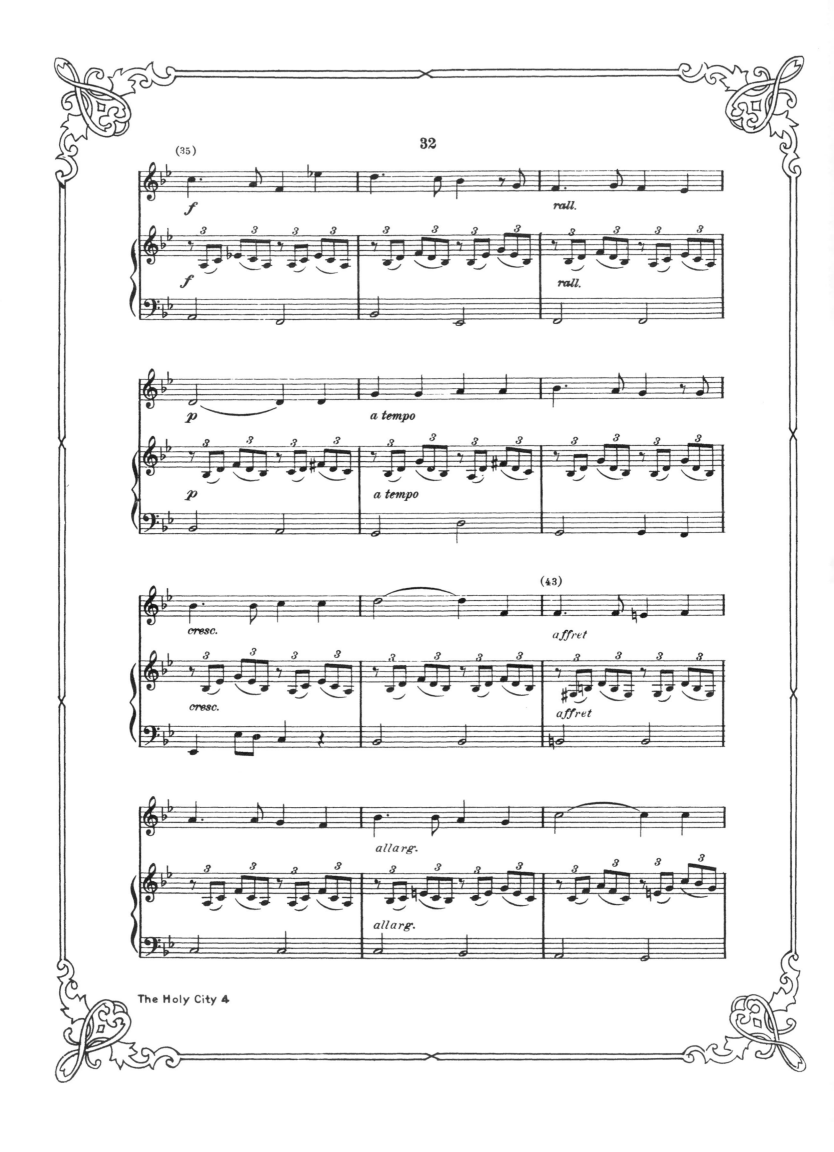

The Holy City 4

Carnival of Venice

Air Varie

Piano

HENRY W. DAVIS

Copyright MCMXLII by Rubank, Inc., Chicago, Ill.
International Copyright Secured

Copyright Renewed

Cor.-Trom.

Cor.-Trom.

Cor.-Trom.

Piano

Gran gusto

Cor.-Trom.

Cor.-Trom.

Cor.-Trom.

GLEN EDEN

POLKA

Piano

CHAS. W. STORM

Copyright Renewed

Copyright MCMXXXIII by Rubank Inc., Chicago, Ill.
International Copyright Secured

41

Cadenza

POLKA

Fine

Fine

p-f

D. S. al Fine

D. S. al Fine

Glen Eden

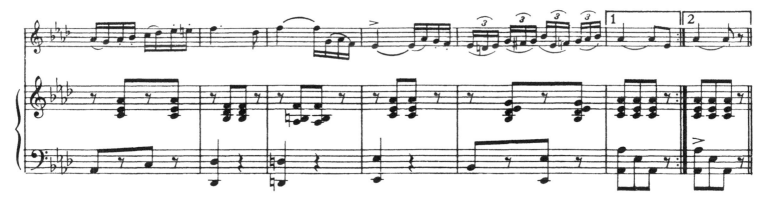

Glen Eden

44
Stupendo
Concert Polka

Piano

N. K. BRAHMSTEDT

Copyright Renewed

Copyright **MCMXXXVII** by Rubank, Inc., Chicago, Ill.
International Copyright Secured

Stupendo - 4

Piano

Polka

Stupendo- 4

Piano

Stupendo- 4